100

Hungry Monkeys!

Masayuki Sebe

Uh-oh! It's lunchtime, and these **100** monkeys are all out of food!

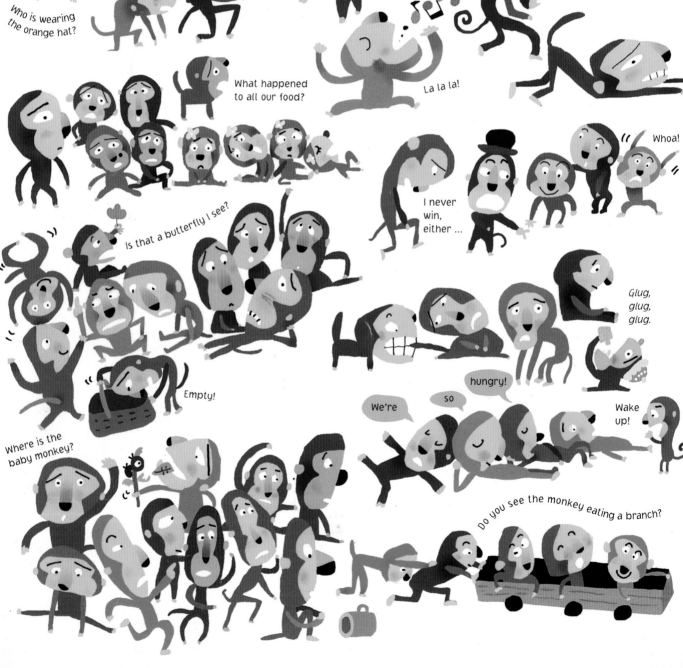

The leader monkey calls the other 99 ...

"Follow me!"

Huh?

I'm so hungry!

Which monkeys are playing Rock, Paper, Scissors?

Waaah!

Where are you going?

Yuck!

Is that tasty?

Which monkey is biting a tail?

Groan!

Oh, dear!

Can you find these things?

Then all **100** hungry monkeys set off to look for something to eat.

These leaves are delicious.
I'll eat anything!
nom, nom, nom ...
Yum!
Huh?
Crunch!
Count the green watermelons.
Who's inside a watermelon?

And **100** excited monkeys find many, many things to eat! Enough for everyone!

Can you find these foods?

Rawwrr!

Oh, no! **100** frightened monkeys are about to become lunch!

Run, monkeys, run!

99 brave monkeys hold on tight as the monster gets closer and closer!

Who has an apple?

Don't let go!

EEK!

Who's the strongest monkey?

Phew! **100** lucky monkeys escape just in time!

15

So **100** strong monkeys work together to pull him up.

I want to help, too!

Whee!

Grunt.

Mmmm ...

How many fruits are in the basket?

Hi!

Neigh!

Which monkey has a spot on his face?

17

19

Mi-mi-mi-miiiiii!
Neigh!
Help me find my wagon!
Who's petting a horse?
Which monkey is already sleeping?
Tra-la-la-la!
Doo-be-doo-be-doo!
La-la-la-la-la!
Chirp! Chirp!
Who's lifting a monkey over his head?

How many monkeys have yellow flowers on their heads?

That night, **100** happy monkeys and the monster gather around the campfire for a sing-along.

Laaaaaaaaaaa!

Ssss ...

Where's the monkey doing a handstand?

Tweet! Tweet!

I can see it now!

What do you see?

Dum-da-dum-da-dum!

Can you find these twigs?

At bedtime, ~~100~~ 99 sleepy monkeys and their new monster friend tuck themselves in.

Goodnight, little monkeys. Goodnight, monster. Tomorrow is another day of play!

Did you see ...

this beetle?
(pages 2-3)

this raven?
(pages 4-5)

this frog?
(pages 6-7)

this ant?
(pages 8-9)

this bird?
(pages 10-11)

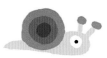

this worm?
(pages 12-13)

this snail?
(pages 14-15)

this bunny?
(pages 16-17)

this whale?
(pages 18-19)

this snake?
(pages 20-21)

this lizard?
(pages 22-23)

Originally published in Japanese under the title *Osaru ga 100-piki* by Kaisei-sha Publishing Co., Ltd.
English translation rights arranged through Japan Foreign-Rights Centre.

Kids Can Press acknowledges the financial support of the Government of Ontario, through the Ontario Media Development Corporation's Ontario Book Initiative.

Published in Canada by
Kids Can Press Ltd.
25 Dockside Drive
Toronto, ON M5A 0B5

Published in the U.S. by
Kids Can Press Ltd.
2250 Military Road
Tonawanda, NY 14150

www.kidscanpress.com

English edition edited by Caitlin Drake Smith and Yvette Ghione

This book is smyth sewn casebound.
Manufactured in Malaysia, in 10/2013, by Tien Wah Press (Pte) Ltd.

CM 14 0 9 8 7 6 5 4 3 2 1

Library and Archives Canada Cataloguing in Publication

Sebe, Masayuki, 1953–
 [Osaru ga 100-piki. English]
 100 hungry monkeys! / written and illustrated by Masayuki Sebe.

Translation of: Osaru ga 100-piki.
ISBN 978-1-77138-045-4 (bound)

1. Counting — Juvenile literature. 2. Monkeys — Juvenile literature.
I. Title. II. Title: One hundred hungry monkeys. III. Title: Osaru ga 100-piki. English.

QA113.S443 2014   j513.2'11   C2013-904448-5

Kids Can Press is a CORUS™ Entertainment company